Assertiveness Style Profile

Dr. Jon Warner

HRD Press • Amherst • Massachusetts

Published by: HRD Press, Inc.
                22 Amherst Road
                Amherst, MA 01002
                (800) 822-2801 (U.S. and Canada)
                (413) 253-3488
                (413) 253-3490 (Fax)
                http://www.hrdpress.com

In association with Team Publications.

ISBN: 0-87425-708-5

Cover design by Eileen Klockars
Production services by Anctil Virtual Office

Assertiveness Style Profile

The Assertiveness Style Profile is designed to assist individuals to understand their own personal assertiveness style, preferences, and behavior, and in so doing, give them a basis to look at ways in which to look at how they might make adjustments to achieve better results for them in the future.

Everyone has their own unique assertiveness style, and there are therefore no right or wrong answers in terms of which individual approach is "best" or more appropriate than any other. In fact, as you will see in this instrument, people will usually score in all four broad assertiveness styles, which means that they will draw upon a little or a lot of each when they meet with other people or groups.

The data provided by this instrument will only be valid and useful if the person completing the questions is as honest as possible and focuses on what they **actually** tend to do and **not** what they think they should be doing in the future.

This is a self-scoring profile. Once you have completed all the statements, you will be given instructions on how to plot your scores on the effective assertiveness grid shown on page 13. This will give you a diagrammatic representation of your current assertiveness style and behavior, as well as suggest where the "average" effective assertiveness styles lie. Some general interpretative information is then included in the back of this booklet to help individuals to determine whether future changes in their style could increase their personal effectiveness and the quality of the results that they achieve.

DIRECTIONS

On the following page, you will find 32 statements about assertiveness. For each statement, think about how you currently behave in real situations now (not guess how you should act in the future). In some cases, a statement will be "TRUE" of your current style and in some cases it will be "FALSE." However, to provide a wider scale of applicability, you should choose the answer that most closely fits your view from the following:

T	**True for you**
PT	**Partly true for you**
N	**Neither true nor false for you** (try to avoid this choice if you can)
PF	**Partly false for you**
F	**False for you**

Please use a ballpoint pen or hard pencil and mark your answers clearly on the Response Form.

Assertiveness Style: Questions

1. I often openly disagree with people when they express an opinion that is different to mine.

2. I will often just take the blame for something rather than to make excuses.

3. I gently address issues that are important to me if people seem to be pleasant and friendly.

4. I feel very comfortable declining offers from even persuasive sales representatives.

5. Some confrontations in which I become involved remain unresolved.

6. I avoid questioning or approaching people when they cut in front of me in line.

7. I don't feel embarrassed or inhibited at showing or being shown affection.

8. I don't mind often asking colleagues or friends for favors.

9. I always strongly persevere in getting my ideas heard and acted upon.

10. The meek will inherit the earth.

11. I try to empathize with everyone I encounter.

12. I cope quite calmly with aggressive outbursts.

13. Given just cause, I will publicly criticize or admonish people.

14. When someone is angry, I often stay silent and just listen and watch.

15. I like to wait for a good moment to get my message across properly.

16. If I'm owed something, I give my debtor a friendly reminder.

17. I sometimes try to stare people down.

18. I find it easy to stay calm and unemotional when people put me under pressure.

19. I am relaxed and easy going in relating to people.

20. I openly and comfortably acknowledge that others might have different views from mine.

21. I often interrupt people or talk over the top of them.

22. I often find myself reflecting mentally on other people's words or behaviors.

23. I give and receive a lot of information when socializing.

24. I typically will not accept poor service.

25. It is always better to speak your mind whatever the risk.

26. I rarely make a fuss even if I know I am being manipulated.

27. In order to get people to more effectively listen, I build the quality of the relationship.

28. When I make mistakes, I admit to them without feeling guilty or inept.

29. I can get annoyed or lose my temper when people criticize me.

30. I like watching the actions of other people when they get excited or highly animated.

31. I aim to use language that will appeal to the other person(s) I'm trying to influence.

32. I tell people about my rights or personal expectations when necessary.

Introduction

Assertiveness is a communication philosophy and technique. It involves interacting with others in a confident and persistent manner, particularly when there is an element of conflict present.

Assertive people:

- Feel empowered. They do not feel unjustly controlled by others.
- Are proactive. That is, they make things happen and are not reactive, or always waiting to respond to the words and actions of others.
- Know their rights and responsibilities in dealing with others.
- Are able to resist aggressive, manipulative, and passive ploys of other people.

A good definition of assertiveness is:

Getting what you want from others without infringing upon their rights

The model on the following page has a two axis grids. One axis describes the **level of "energy"** that an individual might adopt in a situation in which they are communicating with one or more people. This runs from "Strong" to "Gentle." This usually means verbal energy in terms of speaking (when the voice may be louder and more forceful), but it also has associated non-vocal characteristics such as leaning forward, high use of other body language and/or facial expressions, etc.

The other axis on the grid relates to the **level of "empathy"** that may be preferred by an individual. This runs from "Warm" to "Cool."

By intersecting these two axes, the grid created shows four assertiveness styles. Every one of these four styles may be adopted in different situations, although it is likely that most individuals will stick to their greatest preference in most circumstances they encounter.

Of course, all of these styles have their associated strengths and weaknesses, and some are more useful and applicable in different circumstances than others. The diamond shape or shaded area shows how much of each quadrant in the grid is typically used for a positively assertive individual. Don't forget these are only averages, not fixed recipes for all people in all circumstances. Although the level of energy should be a little higher than average, it is the empathy side of the grid that assertiveness is often shown.

Firm and positive assertiveness requires considerable practice for many people. However, it is fair to say that successful efforts to be assertive often arise from a strong feeling of self worth or high self esteem combined with a strong and positive belief about the intrinsic worth or value of others around you.

Four "Assertiveness Styles"

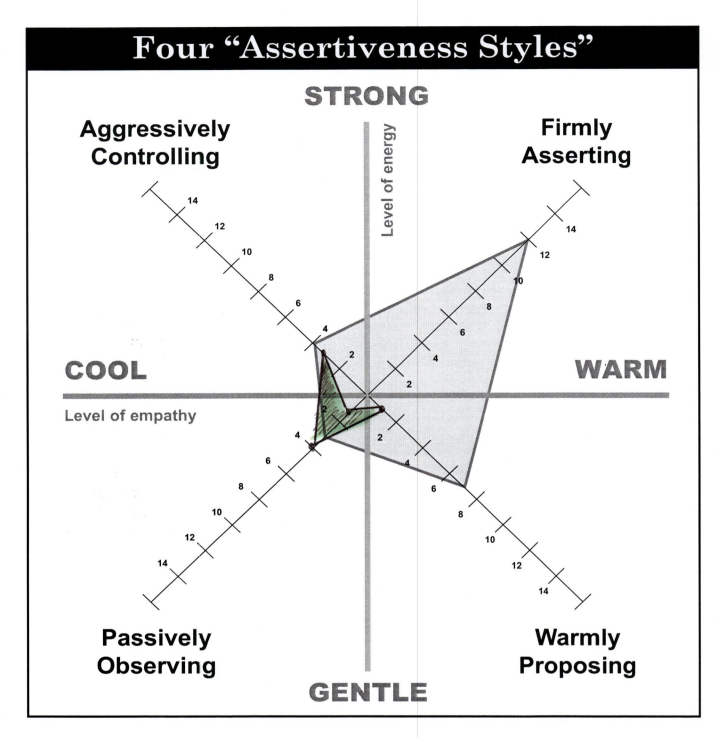

The diamond-shaped shaded area suggests how much of each quadrant is used most consistently to achieve successful results, by being suitably assertive in most situations. Of course, every communication circumstance is different and might require slightly different styles to handle it. This graph "shape" is therefore only an "average" and merely suggests that we should steer away from aggressive and passive styles if we want to become more assertive.

Scoring Your Instrument

By peeling the carbonated scoring sheet from the response sheet, you will see that your T, PT, N, PF and F responses have translated into both positive and negative numbers. Your first task is to total these numbers and enter them in the appropriate column sum boxes at the foot of the page. Care should be taken to add positive and negative numbers carefully. You may therefore end up with an overall score that is positive or negative or even zero (with all the positives and negatives netting out).

The four column sums (**Aggressively Controlling, Passively Observing, Warmly Proposing,** and **Firmly Asserting**) correspond to each quadrant in the assertiveness grid. By translating these total column scores, you can now plot these numbers on the grid by making a mark on the relevant diagonal axis counting outward from the center. Each scale runs from 0 at the center to 16 at the end of the scale on the positive side (and has progression points at 2, 4, 6, 8, 10, 12, and 14). The scale is also 0 to 16 on the other or the negative side of the diagonal. If your score on Aggressively Controlling (for example) is negative, your mark should be made on the diagonal line in the Warmly Proposing quadrant.

Although most people will have a net positive score in all four quadrants, some people will have a net positive score in only three or possibly two quadrants. This simply means that they are highly unlikely to ever use the quadrants in which they do not score at all (in a communication situation) from their answers.

Once you have all four points from your four column scores plotted on the grid, connect all four points with a straight line with your pen or pencil, and shade in the resultant shape. You can review this shape in terms of which quadrant has the greatest area (your primary indicated assertiveness style) and the next largest (your secondary indicated assertiveness style), and so on.

Finally, you can compare the shape of your assertiveness style "diamond' with the most commonly used style in order to be positively assertive (the diamond shape grey-shaded on the grid). This shape is suggested to be the style that most consistently achieves the best results in most (but not all) situations, or in circumstances in which being more assertive will achieve better outcomes.

An example of an individually scored grid is shown on the following page.

Plotting Your Assertiveness Style

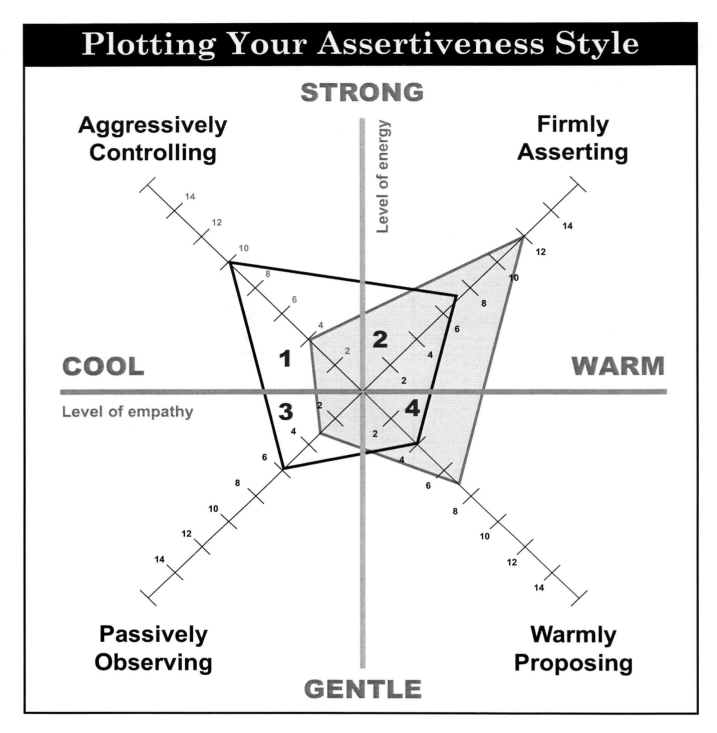

The individual diamond has the greatest shaded area in the **Aggressively Controlling** quadrant (their primary style) followed by the **Firmly Asserting** quadrant (their secondary style). The **Passively Observing** style is also stronger than the **Positive Assertiveness** average. This individual might like to look at developing their assertiveness style in the "warm" side of the grid and make **less** use of the **Aggressively Controlling** style in some future discussions or meetings with people.

Interpreting Your Results

The effective assertiveness grid has four quadrants, which carry four 'labels'. These are:

1. **Aggressively controlling**
2. **Passively observing**
3. **Warmly proposing**
4. **Firmly asserting**

These quadrants are the outcome descriptions from the level of energy and the level of empathy used in assertiveness. This is represented on two intersecting axes in a simple grid fashion as follows:

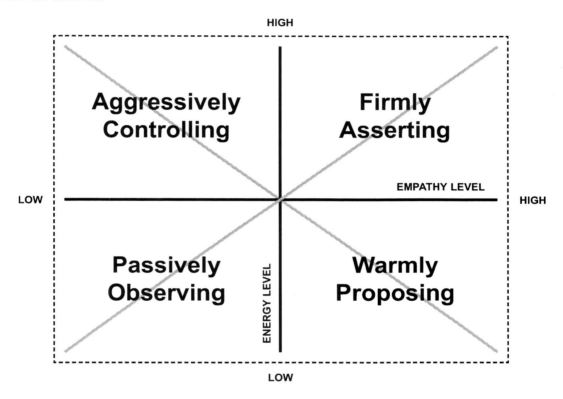

Individuals might actually draw on all four of these different communication styles in the same communication, or in different situations from time to time. In addition, an individual can learn or choose to use more of a particular style than another. However, if the instrument has been completed honestly, for the most part, an individual is likely to have a primary and/or a secondary style that are considerably stronger than the others. This means that they are likely to adopt these styles more often and with greater ease than other styles.

Each assertiveness style has its inherent strengths and weaknesses, depending upon the person, the other party or parties in the discussion, and the type of communication to take place. Let's look at each of these styles in more detail (although it should be remembered that these descriptions relate to high scores in these quadrants—usually 8 or more. Lower scores will have only some of the characteristics described.

The Four Assertiveness Styles

AGGRESSIVELY CONTROLLING

In this high energy, low empathy quadrant, the individual is likely to literally want to be in control in most of their encounters or conversations with others. To do this, they might consciously or unconsciously "trample" on the rights of others. This style can therefore be very direct and commanding of attention. Individuals using this style fail to listen to others or regularly interrupt them when speaking. This style will also make high use of strong body language and a loud and confident voice (to effect the control being sought). The pros and cons of this style are shown on the following page.

Likely Body Language: Invades space, loud voice, arms crossed or moving in aggressive manner (like pointing), and very direct eye contact or even staring.

FIRMLY ASSERTING

In this high energy, high empathy quadrant, the individual is likely to have a feeling of high self worth and a good understanding of their personal needs and rights. However, they also recognize and value the important needs that others have. As such, this style will usually listen to others attentively before firmly communicating their message, or to outline what they need in the context of what they have heard. This style is also likely to have strong personal standards and act to ensure that these are compromised as little as possible. The pros and cons of this style are shown on the following page.

Likely Body Language: Relaxed, slightly leaning forward posture, lots of use of the hands, good eye contact, and confident, usually modulated voice.

PASSIVELY OBSERVING

In this low energy, low empathy quadrant, the individual is likely to keep to themselves or to remain quiet and unassuming in most discussions or meetings with others. This style is happy to watch the antics of others in a detached way, without feeling the need to join in or to enter the discussion. When directly engaged, this style is likely to often give way or concede to more aggressive types, but to mentally analyze how they might redress the balance in a different way in the future. The pros and cons of this style are shown on the following page.

Likely Body Language: Leaning back, hands clasped or arms crossed, eyes averted or watching the broad scene with fleeting looks and possible sighs.

WARMLY PROPOSING

In this low energy, high empathy quadrant, the individual is likely to offer gentle comments and suggestions in discussions and conversations. This style is generally more interested in finding out about other people and in building better relationships. They will therefore be unlikely to jeopardize a positive conversational climate to push even their important points too hard. They might therefore accept that they may not get everything they seek in a discussion, but there is always the next time. The pros and cons of this style are shown on the following page.

Likely Body Language: Open posture, attentive, good eye contact, friendly, smiling face, some use of hands when speaking, and concentrating, so as to listen properly.

Of these four styles, data gathered to date suggests that it is the Firmly Asserting style that is used the most and is adopted more than any other by people who are seen to be the most positive in their efforts to be assertive (and who are happy with the end result of their efforts). This is followed by the Warmly Proposing style, the Aggressively Controlling style, and the Passively Observing style last. It should be noted, however, that this is only an averaged finding. It needs to therefore be remembered that each situation might see the use of a different mix of styles each time.

Assertiveness Style Pros and Cons

STRONG

Aggressively Controlling

PRO	CONS
• Is commanding and confident when required to be.	• Is often insensitive to the rights and needs of others. • Might adopt a sarcastic or hostile attitude. • Interrupts and talks over others without listening.

Firmly Asserting

PROS	CON
• Takes action toward getting what is wanted without denying others' rights. • Proactive and solution oriented to always find a positive way forward. • Demonstrates that they value people's feelings and others' needs. • Listens well.	• Might not coach others who are less assertive.

HIGH

Level of energy

COOL

WARM

LOW   Level of empathy   **HIGH**

Passively Observing

PROS	CONS
• Effectively analyzes discussions or debates. • Can listen well.	• Ignores/sacrifices own rights. • Stays silent rather than speaking up. • Can feel inept at times.

Warmly Proposing

PROS	CONS
• Keeps the discussions and conversations calm and friendly. • Gently offers lots of ideas and suggestions.	• Might not come to the point about what they want or need. • Might become upset in the face of high aggression or anger.

LOW

GENTLE

Your Individual Score

Once you have plotted your individual score, as long as this has been done honestly and accurately, you should be in a position to:

1. **Review the balance of styles that you draw upon when you engage in communication (at the moment).**
2. **Compare your mix of assertiveness styles with the effective assertiveness average diamond-shaped profile.**
3. **Determine whether you should look to adjust your style or to practice making more use of styles other than your current primary style to achieve better future results.**

As we said at the outset, there are no right or wrong answers in assertiveness. This is partly because every situation is highly individualistic. As such, every person needs to try to use the style that is both comfortable for them and is likely to work in the particular situation. After all, assertiveness with someone you may have known for a long time as a friend is likely to be quite different from the sort of assertiveness you might need when you want to stand up to someone in a store who has been rude to you. You would likely use the **Warmly Proposing** assertiveness style with your friend and perhaps the **Aggressively Controlling** or **Firmly Asserting** assertiveness style with the person in the store.

In the final analysis, the essential value in any measurement instrument is in the extent to which it provides a useful indicator of your personal way of operating. This should ideally be helpful in a way that individuals can reflect upon and judge whether any adjustments or changes are necessary or desirable.

By completing this profile, the intensity of your scores should provide a useful basis for such a review to take place. To deepen or extend this further, you may want to ask two or three of your colleagues to complete the profile as they see your assertiveness style. By averaging their scores and plotting them on the grid, this can create an interesting comparison between your own perceived personal style and the style that others perceive you to practice when they see you trying to be more assertive.

Whatever your scores, and whether they are yours alone or enhanced by the views of others, you might want to develop your skills in quadrants other than the one in which you are already strongest (your primary style). Consequently, on the following page, you will find a number of broad suggestions that you might like to think about in each category.

Suggestions for Developing Assertiveness Skills

The following are general suggestions that can be taken to make greater positive use of each of the four assertiveness styles. Bear in mind that you are likely to be more successfully assertive the more you use the **Firmly Assertive** quadrant over all the others in most situations.

AGGRESSIVELY CONTROLLING	FIRMLY ASSERTING
Positive ways to use this style: 1. Make your points more directly in a louder, more confident voice. 2. State your rights strongly to others.	**Positive ways to use this style:** 1. Develop your attentive listening skills. 2. Find ways to empathize with the other person or persons or "put yourself in their shoes." 3. Confidently, clearly, and firmly state your own needs and expectations to others. 4. Aim to be flexible to adapt your position to protect your own rights and avoid infringing on the rights of others. 5. Look for opportunities to find approaches that represent a good outcome for both parties.
PASSIVELY OBSERVING	WARMLY PROPOSING
Positive ways to use this style: 1. Aim to quietly look for the underlying reasons or motivations for the points made by the others as they talk. 2. Learn to watch and interpret body language more often. 3. Use constructive silence to help you reflect more often in conversations.	**Positive ways to use this style:** 1. Try to play the role of calm and friendly offerer of ideas and suggestions. 2. Bring people into conversations through small talk more often. 3. Find out more about other people's needs and aspirations and focus on those that match your own. 4. Look to explain your points carefully and in a gentle and assured way.

A Few Quotations Applicable to Assertiveness

AGGRESSIVELY CONTROLLING	FIRMLY ASSERTING
• If aggressors are wrong above, they are right here below. *Napoleon* • You must either conquer and rule or serve and lose, suffer or triumph, be the anvil or the hammer. *Goethe* • Speak when you are angry and you will make the best speech you will ever regret. *Ambrose Bierce* • It is not necessary to understand things in order to argue about them. *Pierre Beaumarchais* • When your argument has little or no substance, abuse your opponent. *Cicero*	• Respect yourself if you would have others respect you. *Baltasar Gracian* • To be a hero, one must give an order to oneself. *Simone Weil* • If you think you can or you think you can't, you're right. *Henry Ford* • No-one can make you feel inferior without your consent. *Eleanor Roosevelt* • To know oneself, one should assert oneself. *Albert Camus*
PASSIVELY OBSERVING	**WARMLY PROPOSING**
• Beware of one who flatters unduly; he will also censure unjustly. *English Proverb* • Whoever gossips to you will gossip of you. *Spanish Proverb* • Better an open enemy than a false friend. *English Proverb* • The cruellest lies are often told in silence. *Robert Louis Stevenson* • Deceive not thy physian, confessor, nor lawyer. *George Herbert* • No man has a good enough memory to make a successful liar. *Abraham Lincoln*	• He that cannot ask, cannot live. *English Proverb* • He that asks faintly begs a denial. *English Proverb* • Whosoever shall smite thee on thy right cheek, turn to him the other also. *Bible, Matthew 5:39* • Hatred is the coward's revenge for being intimidated. *George Bernard Shaw* • Strong men can always afford to be gentle. Only the weak are intent on "giving as good as they get." *Elbert Hubbard*

Your Assertiveness Grid Profile

Name: _____ Date: _____

STRONG

Level of energy

Aggressively
Controlling

Firmly
Asserting

14
12
10
8
6
4
2

14
12
10
8
6
4
2

COOL

WARM

Level of empathy

2

4
6
8
10
12
14

2
4
6
8
10
12
14

Passively
Observing

Warmly
Proposing

GENTLE

Note: The diamond-shaped shaded area suggests how much of each quadrant is used most consistently to achieve successful results by being suitably assertive. However, this is only a suggested and averaged shape. Each situation will obviously require a slightly different emphasis according to the circumstances.

ABOUT THE AUTHOR

Jon Warner is a professional manager with over 20 years' experience working with multinational companies in the United Kingdom, Europe, the United States, and Australia. He has been the senior staff member in human resources departments, and has held several professional leadership positions with responsibility for large groups of employees. Jon has in recent years been involved in wide-ranging organizational consultancy work and the pursuit of best-practices leadership for such major organizations as Mobil Oil, Quantas, United Energy, Dow Corning, Coca Cola, Barclays Bank, National Bank, Honda, BTR, Gas and Fuel, Air Products and Chemicals, and Caltex.

Jon is managing director of Team Publications PTY Limited, an international training and publishing company committed to bringing practical and fun-to-use learning material to the worldwide training market, such as the One Page Coach® storyboard-based integrated training packages. He holds a master's degree in Business Administration and a Ph.D. in organizational change and learning, and lives and works on Australia's Gold Coast.

Gary Jenkins is an experienced writer and author of numerous books and manuals in the area of personal and organizational learning and change. Most of Gary's work has been in the educational sector in the United Kingdom, but he has consulted to a wide variety of organizations in the United Kingdom, Europe, the United States, and Australia.

Gary started his degree in Philosophy and Politics at Hull University, but later switched to English language and American studies. He now lives and works in Exeter in Devon in the United Kingdom.

REFERENCES

Burley-Allen, M. 1995. *Managing Assertively: A Self-Teaching Guide* (Second Edition). New York: John Wiley and Sons.

Eunson, B. 1997. *Dealing With Conflict.* Brisbane: John Wiley and Sons.

Fritchie, R. and M. Melling. 1991. *The Business of Assertiveness.* London: BBC Books.

Jakubowski, P. and A. J. Lange. 1978. *The Assertive Option: Your Rights and Responsibilities.* Champaign, Illinois: Research Press.

Schwimmer, L. D. 1980. *How to Ask for a Raise Without Getting Fired and 24 Other Assertiveness Techniques for the Office.* San Francisco: Harper and Row.